Praise for *Revolution Today*

"Susan Buck-Morss in *Revolution Today* offers people across the globe a newer way of seeing, knowing, acting, and naming their political engagements. She uses extraordinary images to assist us in articulating newly robust revolutionary imaginings. As always, Susan finds history in the present without its limitations. It's a stunning read for these urgent times."

—Zillah Eisenstein, writer, activist, and professor emerita of anti-racist feminist theory, Ithaca College

REVOLUTION TODAY

Susan Buck-Morss

Praise for Susan Buck-Morss

"Susan Buck-Morss is a researcher who scrutinizes the porous boundaries of the systems of meanings and looks for cracks in the seemingly cohesive modern narration on freedom, emancipation, and humanity. She reaches beyond the specialized languages of individual disciplines, on which she draws and which she mixes, and intently observes visual culture."

—*Political Critique*

REVOL

UTION TODAY

Susan Buck-Morss

Haymarket Books
Chicago, Illinois

Published in 2019 by
Haymarket Books
P.O. Box 180165
Chicago, IL 6618
773-583-7884
www.haymarketbooks.org
info@haymarketbooks.org

ISBN: 978-1-60846-679-5

Distributed to the trade in the US through Consortium Book Sales and Distribution
(www.cbsd.com) and internationally through Ingram Publisher Services International
(www.ingramcontent.com).

This book was published with the generous support of
Lannan Foundation and Wallace Action Fund.

Cover design by Rachel Cohen.
Interior design by Eric Kerl.

Printed in Canada by union labor.

Library of Congress Cataloging-in-Publication data is available.

2 4 6 8 10 9 7 5 3 1

Contents

Introduction

THE YEAR 2017–18 marked a confluence of political anniversaries. It was the centennial of the October 1917 revolution that brought the Bolsheviks to power in Russia. It was the fiftieth anniversary of May '68, the Paris student/workers' revolt that had iterations throughout the world. Marx's *Capital*, volume 1, was 150 years old. And Marx himself turned 200 in May 2018. Conferences were convened globally to reflect on the question: What has become of the left revolutionary project? For most of the twentieth century, Marxism served as the common political language of the left. In every nation, his critical texts were translated, read, debated, and practiced. Revolutionary movements in Marx's name were multiple. From China to Cuba they achieved success. Marxist networks were a serious challenge to the territorial organization of nation states. International solidarity among revolutionaries threatened to topple state regimes around the world.

Today, on the surface of things, nothing could seem less likely. Capitalism has morphed into a global system of interdependency that overpowers nation states. Populations are pressured into compliance with capital's iron laws. Right-wing populism is on the rise. Neoliberals boast of global hegemony. Individuals are incorporated directly into the capitalist logic of competition, self-promotion, and profit-maximizing that appears both desirable and inevitable. Ironically, the government of China, which claims a monopoly over Marx's legacy, is rising precipitously under conditions of global capitalism, a trajectory that shows no signs of directional change.

The mood on the left fluctuates, toggling between triumph and despair. The critical analysis of the systemic nature of capitalism has never seemed more accurate. Yet, the emergence of a revolutionary subject is not to be found in classical Marxist terms. Left-wing melancholia is on the rise, as is fear of fascism's resurgence. But something crucial is missing from this pessimistic evaluation. Outside the traditional Marxist frame, mobilizations of opposition are not only happening, they are also gaining support, and developing a global consciousness in the process. This is a cause for hope. The fact that the new social movements do not fit the expected left-course of history is not reason for dismissing them—just the opposite, as

1

empirical history shows us that the expected course was wrong. In our time, new political subjects are emerging. This book celebrates their birth.

A celebration requires gifts. This book is a small one. It does not approach a comprehensive theoretical overview or a compendium of political history. It does not take up the ongoing debates that dominate the academic discussion. It is a more personal contribution, based on lived experiences. And for my life, the decentering, multifocal processes of globalization have been as determining as they were unexpected. The trans-local connections generated by globalization have transformed the content of reflection and revolutionized its mediated forms. Recorded here are reflections on small fragments of recent history, the ones that I happen to know. I try to read these fragments through the images they produce and the global messages they contain. Many are credited to leftist organizations whose work is exemplary. They remind us of the potential for global action that already exists and how much of the new revolutionary vernacular we share.

This book emerged out of a series of presentations during the year of revolutionary anniversaries. Material was added each time to address the particular situation: Buenos Aires; London; Moscow; St. Petersburg; São Paulo; Athens; New York City; Middlebury, Vermont.

The particular contexts produced discussions that exposed the limits of my perspective. They underlined the fact that theory is always local, and perceptions of reality are patchy at best. But they also convinced me that the underlying contradiction between nation-state politics and global capitalism is fundamental to our local situations, so that focusing on it can provide a point of convergence. The new subjectivities occupy this point.

I am indebted to the people who organized the meetings I attended during the 2017–2018 anniversary year. Their work and the contributions of other participants shape my thinking and inspire my hope: Mariano López Seoane, NYU Buenos Aires and Daniel Link, Universidad Nacional de Tres de Febrero, organizers of the international conference "Pasado de Revoluciones" in Buenos Aires; Matthew Walker and the Clifford Symposium, "The Soviet Century: 100 Years of Revolution" at Middlebury College; Jodi Dean, Artemy Magun, Alexei Penzin, and Oxana Timofeva, hosts of the international conference, "1917–2017: Revolutions, Communist Legacies and Spectres of the Future" at the European University of St. Petersburg; Judith Butler of the International Consortium of Critical Theory and Vladimir Pinheiro Safatle, Universidade de São Paulo, conveners of the conference "The Ends of Democracy: Populist Strategies, Skepticism about Democracy and the Quest for Popular Sovereignty" in São Paulo; Katherine Carl, curator, and James Sevitt for the series "Reckoning with the Crisis of Imagination" at the St. James Gallery, CUNY Graduate Center; and lecture invitations from Ayça Çubukçu at the London School of Economics, Yiannis Mylonas at the National Research University Higher School of Economics, Moscow, and

Costas Douzinas, member of the Hellenic Parliament in Athens. Thanks as well for the critical feedback provided by my ongoing collective at the CUNY Graduate Center in New York City, the Committee on Globalization and Social Change, directed by Gary Wilder. They are an amazing group of collaborators.

Working with Haymarket has been a pleasure. Thanks to Nisha Bolsey, Anthony Arnove, Caroline Luft, Eric Kerl, and Rachel Cohen. And a final thanks to Zachary Conn, CUNY Graduate Center, for his invaluable assistance with the images.

1. Nation State / Global Capital

The United Nations, founded 1945, New York City headquarters designed by the Brazilian architect Oscar Niemeyer, completed in 1952

THE NATION STATE is not an eternal political form. It became normative as a *global* world order only after World War II. The United Nations headquarters in New York City was its visual manifestation. The victors in the war determined its structure. They included, significantly, the Soviet Union, which exhibited a marked shift toward nationalist goals during and after the war. The exiled national government in Taiwan, rather than the People's Republic on the mainland, acquired Chinese representation. For prewar colonies, the United Nations became the site of struggles for recognition of their independence from European rule. This new geopolitical order appeared incompatible with the Euro-American imperial past. From this time forward, the world was to be organized in terms of nation states. Historically, some would be in advance of others, some would be behind, and others would be fighting wars of *national* liberation, but the ordering form remained dominated by this conceptual imaginary. All international issues after 1950 presumed this national order as the hegemonic norm.

The nation state as an epistemological form captured certain realities but obscured others. It could not recognize the existence of non-state political imaginaries already in existence. This applied not only to socialist internationalism but also to multiple cases where postcolonial political realities had very little to do with boundaries that had been drawn by the colonial powers. [1]

One particularly visionary alternative to the nation-state order was the trans-regional movement of Négritude, which was born in Paris among a diaspora of intellectuals from geographically distant countries in Africa and the Caribbean, and which developed its political theory through literature, poetry, and painting. Négritude's political goal was a transformation of Black consciousness, in the context of which Martinique-born Aimé Césaire and Senegal-born Léopold Senghor rejected the model for anticolonial struggles as national liberation. The goal for Senghor and Césaire was to transform the colonies into equal partners within a decentralized, territorially interdependent, culturally diverse, and democratically governed republic. In our own time of global interconnectedness and multiple diasporas, Négritude's forms of resistant cosmopolitanism seem strikingly relevant.[2] What developed instead were European nations that classified nonwhite and non–native born people as minorities, immigrants, or refugees, and a series of new, postcolonial nations that were equal in name only.

Cover of *The Stages of Economic Growth: A Non-Communist Manifesto*, by W. W. Rostow. The five stages of national growth: (1) Traditional society; (2) Preconditions for takeoff; (3) Takeoff; (4) Drive to maturity; (5) Age of high mass consumption.

---

1.   On the inadequacies of the nation-state form as applied to postcolonial realities, see the PhD dissertation of Mark Drury, "Disorderly Histories: An Anthropology of Decolonization in Western Sahara," (CUNY Graduate Center, 2018).

2.   Gary Wilder, *Freedom Time: Négritude, Decolonization and the Future of the World* (Durham, NC: Duke University Press, 2015).

One of the most blatant examples of the distortions produced by national analyses is in the realm of the economy. In 1960, W. W. Rostow published a highly influential book entitled *The Stages of Economic Growth*. There were five such stages, and all nation states were expected to pass through them as they advanced toward the uncritically accepted goal of a modern-industrialized national economy. The book was subtitled *A Non-Communist Manifesto*; its political purpose was to provide an alternative conception of time to the one that dominated in Marxist discourse: the historically consecutive stages of feudalism and capitalism, leading inevitably to socialism.

To reflect upon how damaging epistemological forms can be, how they can block a clear analysis of what in fact is happening, we need only recall the pathbreaking critique provided by the articulators of dependency theory—writers who challenged the imaginary of nation states *and* the common Marxist variant of inevitable developmental forms. Argentinian-born Raúl Prebisch did the initial empirical research, discovering that the increasing poverty of underdeveloped countries was directly correlated to the increasing wealth of rich nations. This led to important theoretical innovations by a transnational group of scholars: US-born Immanuel Wallerstein, the Brazilians Fernando Henrique Cardozo and Theotonio dos Santos, Enzo Faletto of Chile, and Walter Rodney of Guyana, among others.

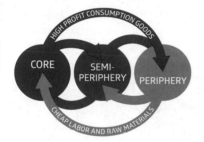

Center-periphery unequal flows

Their work showed that the poverty of the countries in the periphery is not because they lack integration into the world system—they *are* integrated—but a function of how, given that system's structural inequalities. This conceptual shift was profound. The blow to methodological nationalism struck by dependency theory was the precursor to all postcolonial theory that followed. It was subsequently argued that there would have been no rise of Europe without the rise of European colonial occupation, over several centuries, that included the extraction of natural resources, the exploitation of human labor, and accumulation of surplus value in the form of private and national-imperial wealth.

The continued relevance of dependency theory to uneven development of the countries in the European Union is a point of present debate. The questions are: How much have the "core" countries of the EU benefitted from unequal partnership with those of the Global

South, and how responsible is financial capitalism in the core for the economic collapse of southern countries, while the finance capitalists benefit from the austerity programs of debt repayment that have followed? Moreover: How much has nationalist rhetoric destroyed the potential for working-class solidarity in the EU across boundaries of national difference?

Geopolitics in the twenty-first century. Ranking the world's top economies: US—China—Japan—Germany—England—India—France—Brazil

But the geopolitical map is shifting once again, as formerly core regions of the world economy lose their dominance and the powers of global capital continue to expand. These tendencies determine the present historical conjuncture, situating where we are in time.

Because of the hegemony of the nation-state model, which continues to dominate even in the federated economic unit of Europe, the only significant political power that people have today is through the institutions of the specific nation states in which they are citizens. At the same time, and in contradiction to this political ordering, their fates—economically, and in every other way—are tied to those elsewhere. The capacity of national governments to protect their citizens from crises within the global economic order is structurally limited, as Southeast Asia discovered in 1997, Argentina in 2001, the United States in 2008, and Greece in 2015.

Thailand, Silom Road, 1997. The baht has collapsed and a very unpopular IMF is imposing massive restrictions on the country.

March in continuing opposition to the Argentinian government's agreement with the IMF, May 25, 2018

Marchers in the Lawrenceville neighborhood of Pittsburgh, Pennsylvania, on September 24, 2009, protesting the 2009 G-20 Summit

Protest against the Irish government's handling of the financial crisis, February 21, 2009

Greece votes "NO"—OXI—(61 percent) against the austerity demanded by the EU, 2015

As a response to the globalization of the economy, nationalism continues its political appeal. Indeed, it has become more strident. Yet, resistance to global capital cannot be successful at the level of nation states. Nor can national governments resolve other fundamental issues that underlie politics in our time. Questions of war and peace—and now, with increasing significance, issues of climate change and ecological limits—call for *global* solidarity as a political imperative. From the perspective of the world's bio-interrelatedness, all wars today are civil wars. No population of living organisms would survive a nuclear World War III unscathed.

ESTIMATE OF GLOBAL NUCLEAR WEAPONS IN JANUARY 2018

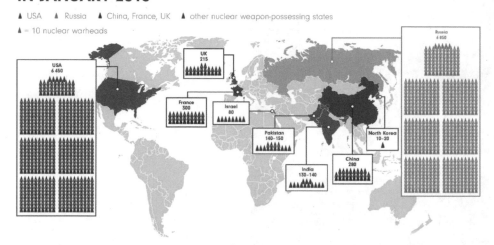

World nuclear forces 2018: countries possessing nuclear weapons, number of warheads worldwide

Polar bears declared threatened species by the US government, May 2008

The post–World War II era has been defined by scientists as the Age of the Anthropocene. Human activity is now the dominant influence on climate and the environment, and the survival of species in the natural world. Seeing the planet in this way makes evident the irrationality of the political world order. The endangered ecosystem and the exclusionary, self-interested policies of nation states are incompatible. Transnational solidarity is a necessity. But can it happen?

"The experience of our generation:
that capitalism will die no natural death."
—Walter Benjamin, *The Arcades Project*

Nothing follows necessarily from the contradictory situation of the present. Yes, capitalism as a system intrinsically leads to crisis. But economic crisis is not a theory of history, and the class struggle does not guarantee redemption. As leftists of Walter Benjamin's generation learned, the global depression of 1929 led to fascism and world war, not human liberation. Glorification of the moment of historical rupture, as if it were itself the political solution, is irresponsibly romantic. At the same time, the presumption that linear projections of the given world will extend indefinitely into the future is empirically naïve. Change does happen, but it cannot be predicted from present consciousness, because consciousness itself alters in time—sometimes more suddenly than anyone had thought possible.

2. Historical Surprises from the Recent Past

We will look briefly at three historical events. While not revolutions, they were surprising shifts in the political situation that changed the epistemological landscape. History exposed the potential for something new, allowing—indeed, forcing—us to see the world differently.

La Moneda Palace, Santiago, Chile, September 11, 1973. Chilean forces under General Pinochet staged a coup against Salvador Allende. During their attack on the presidential palace, Allende died.

The first event is the overthrow of the Allende government in Chile on September 11, 1973. Salvador Allende, openly Marxist, had achieved power through free and fair elections. He led a coalition of parties, the goal of which was a democratic form of socialism that included nationalization of the copper, telecommunications, and finance industries; the breakup of landed estates; and the promise of greater worker control of factory production. This was a socialist revolution through democratic means. Moreover, although it was a national revolution, its leaders were consciously aware of the global realities of economic dependency under the existing hegemony of the United States. Allende's government implemented import substitution policies that were in harmony with center-periphery analyses.

And there was another significant factor in the Chilean experiment. It was the first socialist revolution to make use of the new technologies of network organization that were the prototype for computerized systems. In order to appreciate what this could have meant for the success of socialism, one has to understand how problematic it was within the Soviet Union to manage an entire economy through the means of central planning *without* computer technology. The bureaucracy had to be enormous.

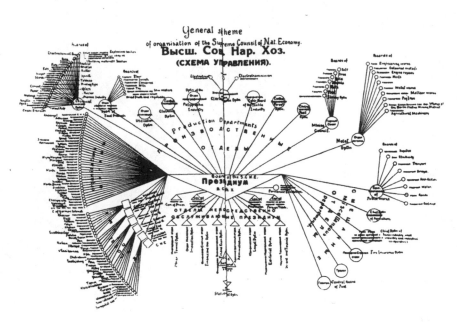

Soviet central planning: "General scheme of organization of the Supreme Council of National Economy." Goods flow into the center for distribution from industrial enterprises producing everything from iron pipes to matchsticks. From *The Russian Economist*, January 1921.

14

During Allende's presidency, a Chilean project called CYBERSYN was instituted by the operations research specialist Stafford Beer, who offered his services to the revolutionary regime. CYBERSYN provided feedback on the economy to the central government in real time.

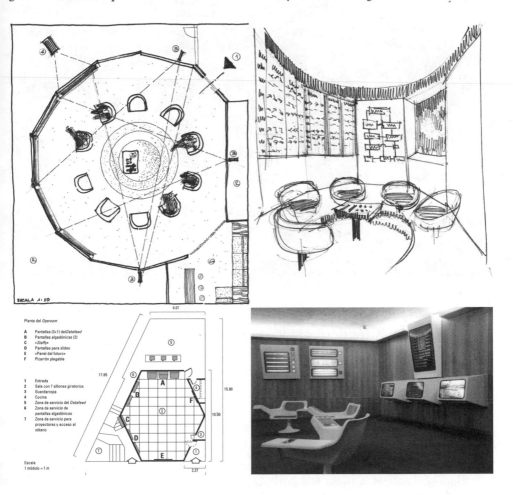

Stafford Beer's design for CYBERSYN

Beer recalls Allende's excitement when he realized that it would be technologically possible for a network of power to truly represent the Chilean people in whose interests he served. Rather than a centralized bureaucracy, Allende envisioned returning decision-making power back to the industrial enterprises as a form of worker self-management.

Stafford Beer design: special operations room—central planning, minimalist style

Three years after taking power, Allende was forcefully removed by a military coup that was supported by the CIA. This was neoimperialism in its most blatant form. In 1976, Allende's former ambassador to the United States, Orlando Letelier, was assassinated in Washington, DC, by a bomb placed in his car, and the US secretary of state, Henry Kissinger, repressed the investigation.[3]

The event of Letelier's funeral became a massive demonstration on the streets of the capital, as ambassadors and the staffs of embassies from countries throughout the Global South joined with US citizens in public protest against the realities of unequal sovereignty among nations and the violent relations of power that structured the US-dominated, self-named Free World.

The overthrow of Allende not only established a brutal military dictatorship under Augusto Pinochet—thousands of citizens were killed by the military—but it also instituted the first systematically neoliberal economic agenda, developed by consultants from Milton

---

3.   This was my personal initiation into the global power realities behind the appearance of the nation-state order. I worked for Orlando as an intern at the Institute for Policy Studies when his assassination occurred. Documents released in 2015 have finally clarified the CIA knew by 1978 that Pinochet had ordered this act. See *Democracy Now!*, interview with Peter Kornbluh, April 12, 2010, https://www.democracynow.org/2010/4/12/new_docs_show_kissinger_rescinded_warning.

Friedman's group at the University of Chicago School of Economics. This deadly mixture of nationalist authoritarianism on the political level and neoliberalism as an economic order would become a prototype for the future. Significantly, it was not the computerized potential of socialist economic planning that destroyed democratically elected socialism in Chile, it was military force with foreign support that ensured the failure of this experiment.

The second unexpected historical event occurred in November 1989, when the Berlin Wall was dismantled by citizen action, demonstrating for the world that sovereign political imaginaries are often less powerful than they appear to be. At a time when the experts were predicting that Germany would stay divided for decades to come, people on the street challenged established wisdom and made another future possible. The lesson this event taught us is that at any moment the logic of the status quo can be disrupted.

Citizens climb over the Berlin Wall, November 10, 1989

In the United States, the myth quickly developed that the wall had fallen miraculously because Ronald Reagan stood in front of it and said: "Mr. Gorbachev, tear down this wall!" Such a causal fantasy ignored the more significant role of Mikhail Gorbachev, who was part of Russia's

'60s generation (the шестидесятники) and had developed Marxist humanist sentiments that looked beyond economic goals. The model of *glasnost'* (гласность) proposed a democratic form of socialism to replace the Communist Party's monopoly of power. This was the most reasonable direction that history *could* have taken. But, despite Hegel's assertion to the contrary, reason is not assuredly the victor in history, and the potential of *glasnost'* remained unrealized.[4]

I recall that post-Soviet intellectuals supported a "third way," particularly in Eastern Europe. They really believed the Western propaganda that equated "free markets" with "free elections," as if capitalism and democracy were linked together by an inner logic that would allow people in the former Soviet republics to have, finally, a "normal life" (нормальная жизнь). They had not taken note of events in Chile under Pinochet, when neoliberalism was first instituted as a conscious political program that proved itself easily compatible with political authoritarianism.

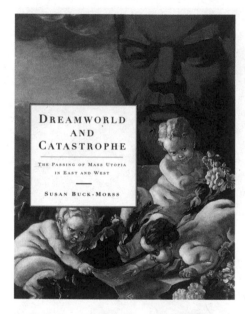

Cover of *Dreamworld and Catastrophe*

At that time I was working together with philosophers from Moscow, Minsk, Warsaw, Sofia, Ljubljana, and Dubrovnik, an experience that led to my writing the book *Dreamworld and Catastrophe: The Passing of Mass Utopia in East and West*. The combined forces of global capitalism and nation-state politics that characterize neoliberalism as a hegemonic structure were then very much in evidence.

---

4. Gorbachev supported a union of republics, not the nationalist separation pushed by Yeltsin (on whose behalf the US meddled in the Russian election of 1996). Gorbachev's proposal for a union might have become a model for the EU.

First, regarding free elections:

Lech Walesa at Gdansk Shipyards, Poland, 1983

The United States was strongly opposed to anything like a "third way." In the first democratic elections in Poland, in 1989, a public relations firm from the United States was active in producing advertisements for democracy that bore no trace of the trade union movement, of the workers themselves, or of their candidate Lech Walesa, who had initiated Polish democracy from below. The US public relations firm produced this poster, with the American Western movie hero Gary Cooper (not Lech Walesa) holding a ballot instead of a gun, as the symbol for change:

Polish election poster, 1989

19

Second, regarding free markets:

United States economists went to Eastern Europe and the former Soviet Union while the populations were experiencing extraordinary economic deprivation. This time it was macro-economists from Harvard (including Jeffrey Sachs), who developed the method of economic "shock therapy"—the Big Bang! Populations were told that they only had to *believe* that "free markets will work" in order, as one advocate wrote, to be brought, "at the other end of the valley of tears, into the sunlight of Western freedom and prosperity."[5] The imposition of economic austerity, which has since become standard within nation states experiencing capitalist crisis, led to predictable consequences. Privatization of state assets produced lopsided capitalist development, whereby a new hyper-rich class came into being: the infamous former-Soviet oligarchs who are now a presence among capitalism's global elite.

China has learned some lessons from watching Russia's casino-capitalist explosion. Its position in the global economy has risen to just below that of the US, but, under the continued rule of the Communist Party, the laboring population has been kept under tight control. While modernization has been successful in terms of construction and transportation, pollution in China has reached disastrous proportions, with only recent attempts to control its pervasive effects. Chinese political authoritarianism is committed to global expansion in the name of the Chinese people, yet its national gains have been skewed toward a wealthy elite that integrates willingly into the global capitalist class.

Now, a third event of recent history that surprised us: as a consequence of the collapse of socialism, the United States assumed unquestioned ideological hegemony over the nation state political and neoliberal economic world order. It maintained this role as the dominant global power, until . . .

September 11, 2001, New York City

---

5.   Cited in Buck-Morss, *Dreamworld and Catastrophe: The Passing of Mass Utopia in East and West* (Cambridge, MA: The MIT Press, 2000), 267.

... nine men, armed with paper cutters, the most low-tech form of weapon imaginable, and financed by laundered money, a system developed for the benefit of global capitalists, managed to stage the self-destruction of US power on morning television.

Destruction, aerial view

This iconoclastic act by non-state actors in the global field destroyed the image of US invulnerability, prompting a US response of preemptive war against two nations while it implemented a state of emergency at home to fight a permanent and unresolvable war on terror. It demonstrated the limits for guaranteeing peace within a world divided into nation states. The obsolete response of the US was to declare war on two sovereign nations that bore no direct responsibility for the action, initiating a regional war that has produced millions of refugees, for whom national borders are a threat to their very survival. At the same time, the order of sovereign nations is also out of step with economic realities. The global economy thrives on the power to shift populations, as needs for labor require, while global capital crosses national boundaries with impunity.

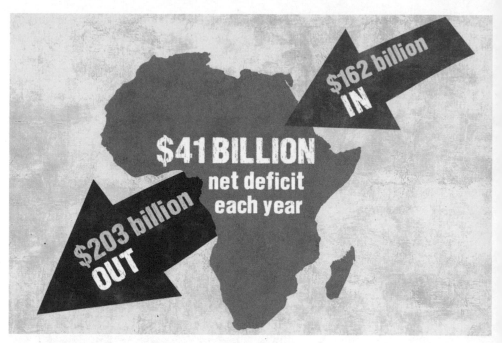

$162 billion
IN

$41 BILLION
net deficit
each year

$203 billion
OUT

This chart for 2014 shows that, as $162 billion flowed into Africa as foreign aid, $203 billion was extracted out of Africa in the form of raw materials, endangered animals, corporate profits, money laundering, tax evasions, and losses in wealth due to climate change—human-caused droughts and famines. Decades after the official end of colonial exploitation, the direction of financial flows is still remarkably prejudiced in favor of the old metropolitan centers, at the expense of the peripheral economies they dominate. The information displayed here is a composite of data from multiple groups that collaborate across national boundaries and who provide a new and necessary education for activists: Health Poverty Action; Jubilee Debt Campaign; World Development Movement; African Forum on Debt and Development (AFRODAD); Friends of the Earth Africa; Tax Justice Network; People's Health Movement, Kenya, Zimbabwe, and UK; War on Want; Community Working Group on Health Zimbabwe; Medact; Healthworkers4All Coalition; groundwork; Friends of the Earth South Africa; and JA! Justiça Ambiental/Friends of the Earth Mozambique.

3. Modernity: A Shared Dream

ONE HUNDRED YEARS after the successful Bolshevik Revolution, we have indeed witnessed the end of an era. But it is not capitalism that has come to an end. Rather it is the dream, shared across the Berlin Wall, of harnessing the powers of industrialization to create a utopia for the masses—in the East through a utopia of production, in the West through a utopia of consumption. This shared dream collapsed two processes, historical progress and economic modernization, into one, and called this single historical trajectory MODERNITY.

Modernity = Modernization = Industrialization

For populations who had not yet attained modernization, time itself was put to task. This was nowhere more true than in the Soviet Union. Lenin recognized that, according to Marxist theory, the socialist revolution ought not to have happened in Russia, which was far "behind" Europe (particularly Germany) and the United States. A certain constraint on freedom was required, he believed, in order to channel revolutionary energies into modernization. Stalin's five-year plans were attempts to push the process forward at an ever faster pace—literally, to accelerate time (ускорение).

USSR in Construction [СССР на стройке], cover by Alexander Rodchenko

Soviet modernization was described as "a race against time"; any political protest questioning the direction of modernization was not allowed because it "slowed down" the course of history. Stalin initiated what has been called the "nationalization of time," over which he had absolute mastery.[6]

Stalin photomontage

The speed of change was itself an act of violence. Stalin put an end to the experimentation of the early Bolshevik artistic avant-garde, in favor of art in direct support of the party vanguard's progress in industrialization. And, most problematically, Soviet planning so completely conflated historical progress with the path the West was taking that there was no questioning of just what kind of modernization was progressive. The forms that modernization was to take followed closely the path of the capitalist West. These included hydroelectric power dams and massive systems for delivery.

---

6.   See Buck-Morss, *Dreamworld and Catastrophe*, 35–39.

Dnieper Hydroelectric Station (from Wikipedia): The DniproHES project used the experience gained from the construction of the Sir Adam Beck Hydroelectric Power Stations at Niagara Falls, Ontario, Canada; the Hydroelectric Island Maligne, Quebec; and the La Gabelle generating station on the St. Maurice River. On September 17, 1932, in recognition for "the outstanding work in the construction of DniproHES," the Soviet government awarded six American engineers (including Hugh Cooper, William V. Murphy, and G. Thompson, engineers of General Electric [who, during the US depression years were hired by the Soviets]), the Order of the Red Banner of Labour.

Interesting for us is the fact that when these dams were being constructed, local energy sources and ideas for solar panels were already being proposed.

Konstantin Melnikov, *Solar Pavilion for the Green City*, 1929

It could indeed be argued that the Soviet experiment failed because it mimicked the models of Western capitalism too faithfully. In retrospect, one can only imagine how far ahead the Soviet Union would have been today if it had chosen to develop alternative forms of modernization, not those that have led to the ecological disasters and global warming that are so threatening to the planet in our time.

But this realization is a recent one. Throughout the twentieth century, there were few places in the world that doubted the dreamworlds of modernization, Western style. When the awakening came, indigenous movements were at the vanguard in producing it. Their desire to conserve their traditional ways of life inspired contemporaries to produce radically original forms of political organization.

Zapatista rebel women

In the 1990s, the Zapatista movement in Chiapas, Mexico, raised global awareness of the truly progressive elements in indigenous traditions. Mayan and Marxist traditions were brought together to create a uniquely powerful revolutionary force, shattering the idea of homogenous, historical time that had provided the organizing frame of modernization. It did so by connecting internationally with civil society activists in a "netwar" against government media suppression, and staging (in 1996) the First Intercontinental Encounter for Humanity, which garnered support worldwide. Movements like the Zapatistas were the political manifestation of a change in consciousness that marked the 1990s, when postcolonial reflection challenged the shibboleth of modernity as progress.

We can track this reversal in the temporal conception through a specific historical example: the attempt to celebrate the five-hundredth anniversary of the first voyage of Christopher Columbus to the lands named by Europeans as the New World.

Plans for this celebration began early. In the 1920s, the Pan-American Union, a US neo-colonial organization that fostered business interests in the Americas, announced a global competition for building a monument to Christopher Columbus in the form of a lighthouse to be constructed in the Dominican Republic, the site of Columbus's first landing.

PROGRAM AND RULES
OF THE
SECOND COMPETITION FOR THE SELECTION
OF AN ARCHITECT FOR

THE
MONUMENTAL LIGHTHOUSE

WHICH THE NATIONS OF THE WORLD
WILL ERECT IN THE DOMINICAN REPUBLIC
TO THE MEMORY OF

CHRISTOPHER COLUMBUS

TOGETHER WITH THE REPORT OF THE
INTERNATIONAL JURY, THE PREMIATED
AND MANY OTHER DESIGNS SUBMITTED
IN THE FIRST CONTEST

Prepared by ALBERT KELSEY, F.A.I.A. Technical Adviser
ISSUED BY THE PAN-AMERICAN UNION
· 1930 ·

Second competition, "The Monumental Lighthouse," 1930

The catalog of finalists for the Columbus Lighthouse Competition was published in 1930, with its headquarters in the imperial metropole of Madrid. The project celebrated Columbus's voyage in space as marking the new era of progress in time. Although the competition announced that "the whole world" had been invited to participate, the second round of semifinalists contained proposals only from Western Europe, the Americas, and the Soviet Union. And although some of the projects included motifs that were described as "Indianism," the predominant aesthetics was the globally shared architecture of modernity. Columbus's voyage of "discovery" was described as "one of the greatest events in the history of the world," one that had a "tremendous" and "vast" influence on civilization, so that "the monument must be one that grips the imagination, one whose appeal is to all time and to all people. . . . It must typify the strength, vision and courage of the man [Columbus], the instrument through whom it was accomplished."[7]

Konstantin Melnikov, 1930. Architectural design among the finalists for the Pan-American Union's competition for a lighthouse to be built in Santo Domingo to celebrate five centuries since Columbus's voyage.

The catalog commented that "architecture to the Communist is another revolutionary weapon, or it would be more just to say, another revolutionary medium of expression":

A struggle for something new—something stronger, simpler, and more vital than any architecture that has gone before, is now taking place in many countries, while in Russia this determined searching and eager experimenting are being carried on with peculiar intensity.

7.   Pan American Union, *Program and Rules of the Second Competition for the Selection of an Architect for the Monumental Lighthouse Which the Nations of the World Will Erect in the Dominican Republic to the Memory of Christopher Columbus* (Washington, DC: Pan American Union, 1930), 5.

The catalog's affirmative attitude toward the Soviet proposal (one of Melnikov's brilliant modernist renditions) reminds us that in this pre–Cold War era, the belief in historical progress was a shared one. At the same time, the catalog's reading of modernity as an aesthetic movement, divorced from its revolutionary political origins, universalized a certain sensibility as abstracted from social change. In this context, Mayan manuscripts could be appreciated for their "precocity in hieratic writing" and "a golden ear of corn (Indian maize)" could adorn the top of a monument's design by the Polish architect Stanislaw Szukalski, while, in a US design, "the future" arose in an "as yet unopened bud of American civilization glowing with a magnificent promise of things greater still to be."[8]

Submission by Polish architect Stanislaw Szukalski

8.   Pan American Union, 114.

The Pan American Union that launched the Columbus Lighthouse Competition had been founded in the 1890s, ushering in the century of US imperialist practices that, in the case of the Americas, entailed an uninterrupted policy of economic domination under the aegis of US military power, as commercial and juridical conflicts were settled in the interests of US firms.

When the five-hundredth anniversary of Columbus's voyage finally came to pass, in 1992, the lighthouse site of Santo Domingo had experienced decades of brutal dictatorship under Rafael Trujillo. Trujillo justified his genocidal massacre of Haitian immigrants and Afro-Dominicans in 1937, known as the Parsley Massacre, as a means of modern nation-building. This was an obscene implementation of nationalism against all other possibilities, producing, by a line of murdered corpses, a physical and racial boundary between Haiti and Santo Domingo where for generations no national boundary had existed. Trujillo's regime achieved what was called peaceful coexistence with the United States. (Franklin Roosevelt's secretary of state, Cordell Hull, famously said that Trujillo "may be a son-of-a-bitch, but he is our son-of-a-bitch.") Trujillo's strongman rule lasted until his assassination in 1961. And when, in 1965, the pro-Castro writer Juan Bosch pulled ahead in presidential elections, the US invaded Santo Domingo with 42,000 troops to prevent what it feared would be a communist outcome.

Santo Domingo, El Faro a Colón, 1992, plans drawn by Scottish architect J. L. Gleave

Columbus Lighthouse, viewed from above

The lighthouse actually constructed was built from the plans of the Scottish architect John Lea Gleave. Light from its center forms the shape of a Christian cross when viewed from the sky. The monument's unveiling in 1992 was marked by local protests, for a number of reasons: the diversion of funds for this project from the needs of the San Dominican population; the fact

that celebrating colonial Spain was an implicit denigration of African Americans and indigenous inhabitants; and the neoimperial history of the Pan American Union's activities. A "Wall of Shame" was proposed, to hide the surrounding poverty. Pope John Paul II cancelled his planned visit. No Latin American republic except Argentina accepted the invitation to attend the unveiling.

The Christopher Columbus Lighthouse monumentalized the spatial imaginary of the West in the drama of history as progress. Some of the original proposals were figural, depicting a ship and including a larger-than-life statue of Columbus. Its realization came too late.

Pan American Union Competition, 1930. Entry of Gino Robuschi, Parma, Italy

31

When the designer Zurab Tsereteli, from post-Soviet Georgia, produced his own version of a monument to Columbus (remarkably similar to his 1997 statue of Peter the Great on the anniversary of three hundred years of the Russian Navy), he had difficulty finding an American port that would accept it. The statue, entitled *Birth of a New World,* finally landed on dry land in Arecibo, Puerto Rico, in 2016, as the "tallest statue in the Western Hemisphere."

Left: Tsereteli's statue of Peter the Great, founder of the Russian navy, in the Neva River Moscow. Right: Tsereteli's monument to Christopher Columbus, *Birth of a New World"* mounted in Arecibo, Puerto Rico. Arecibo is also the location of the National Astronomy and Ionosphere Center, which housed a thousand-foot (305-meter) single-aperture radio telescope. It was the world's largest until July 2016, when a 500-meter aperture spherical telescope (FAST) was completed in China.

4. The Dream Crashes

Symbols of This Century, 1982, by Alexander Kosolapov, Soviet-born artist who emigrated to the US in 1975

A lexander Kosolapov was one of the founders of the Sots Art movement of the 1980s, which merged the styles and content of Soviet political realism with US pop art, as an ironic commentary on both. The artist describes the reception of his image of Lenin and Coca-Cola, white on a red background, which he proposed as symbols of the twentieth century:

THE PROJECT'S STORY

The Russians landed on the moon and painted it red. Then the Americans came and used that red as a background for the Coca-Cola logo. I heard that joke when I was a child.

I designed the Lenin Coca-Cola image in 1980. It was inspired by and addressed to the media. In 1982 it was put out as a postcard, printed first in Paris by Igor Chelkovsky. After that, I published my own edition of Lenin Coca-Cola postcards in New York. The same year I made my first silk screen print of the image.

In November Vladimir Kozlovsky showed the postcard to Richard Pipes, who subsequently brought it to the White House. The same autumn the Lenin Coca-Cola design served as a poster for the group performance of *Kazimir Passion Play* at The Kitchen Performance Center. The poster was seen all over SoHo and was used as a banner over The Kitchen's entrance.

On December 3, a man by the name of Jacques Lang, who posed as an art enthusiast, invited himself to my studio. After viewing my paintings he abruptly introduced himself as a representative of the Coca-Cola company. He told me that an unauthorized use of Coca-Cola logo can result in a lawsuit against me. I saw that I violated the law. On the other hand these kind of laws were totally alien for me as a person brought up in a different world. But the tone of intimidation employed by my visitor was clearly familiar, reminding me of the methods used in my old country. Overcoming the first fright I decided to defend myself. I tried to find a lawyer but soon realized I could not afford one. I was fortunate to have a friendly proposal of Ronald Feldman, who offered me legal assistance by an attorney, Mr. Gerald Rosen, who defended Chris Burden, arrested by the FBI. Mr. Rosen argued that the Coca-Cola is in fact a familiar street sign, which falls in the category of public domain, therefore any artist has the right to utilize it for his/her creative purposes. The Coca-Cola attorney maintained that this particular design hurts his company because it might instill in the American consumer the notion of Coca-Cola Co. promoting communism. (I have always believed that people who are distant from the art have better understanding of it.) Indeed, you can look at the design from the right and see Lenin as a sponsor of Coca-Cola, or look from the left and see Coca-Cola as Lenin's sponsor.

In 1982 I developed the project of a billboard for Times Square. Later, all my attempts to install a Lenin Coca-Cola billboard did not succeed. In 1983 Public Art Fund rejected my proposal with the same response to it in 1985. Privately I was confided that rejection was based on the fact that Coca-Cola was the Fund's sponsor.

In the Perestroyka time it seemed the situation in Moscow became favorable for my project. The Russian Museum was ready to spearhead its fulfillment, and started to raise funds by first approaching the Russian division of Coca-Cola. The response was a prompt "No," with a statement that the company has no money.

Since 1982 on, this work of mine has been one of the most frequently mentioned in the context of the contemporary Russian art.

—Alexander Kosolapov, "The Story of Lenin and Coca-Cola"

Proposal for "Billboard for Times Square," by Alexander Kosolapov

Kosolapov then proposed to situate this most famous image of Lenin and Coca-Cola in a Times Square context that also included a billboard of US founding father George Washington, "Father Knows Best," and another billboard transforming the name of Castro, the founder of modern Cuba, into US vernacular: Castro Convertibles are a brand of fold-out sofa beds.

If *modernity* describes the five-hundred-year period of the history of European expansion that began in 1492, with the myth of the discovery of a new world by Christopher Columbus, ushering in the *longue durée* of coloniality, then not only is the era of modernity over in an empirical sense—the failure of socialist modernization marks this breaking point—but modernity is over as a shared imaginary, a political hope, a utopian dream.

This photo is of Brasília, the new capital city of Brazil, founded in 1960. The construction of this city, a creation *ex nihilo*, was completed in forty-one months as part of the government's plan to compress fifty years of growth into five—echoing Stalin's five-year plans. It represents a highpoint of the shared dream of modernization-as-progress.

Brasília, city buildings designed by the architect Oscar Niemeyer

Guanabara, Brazil, 2015

This photo is of the polluted baywaters of Guanabara, the site of the 2016 Olympic Games in Rio de Janeiro. Brazil, of course, is not unique in this regard. Whether the pollution is of the oceans, the land, or the air, no matter where it begins or how it spreads, the catastrophic results are shared by the world. And responsibility for solutions must be as well.

Seacoast, Guyana, 2010

South End, Hawaii

Philippines

The violence of forced modernization wreaked havoc not only on the environment but also on the diversity of cultures. And so we need not lament the passing of the dream-worlds of modernity. They were dismissive of non-European civilizations and were, at least implicitly, racist.

University of Wisconsin–Madison Chicano students protest the celebration of the five-hundredth anniversary of Columbus's landing in the Americas

Left: Christopher Columbus claims new world

Right: Lakota delegation at the White House, 1877

Any desire to return to the good old days of the hegemony of capitalist America or Stalinist Russia is simply a bad case of nostalgia.

At the same time, it cannot be denied that the *idea* of modernity had enormous power. It shaped the aspirations of people worldwide. Human beings believed that there was no limit to what science could accomplish—combatting sickness, eliminating poverty, eliminating distances, landing on the moon. The rivalry between capitalist modernity and socialist modernity was only about the means, not the end, of the dream of human progress. In that sense, modernity could lay legitimate claim to universality as its goal.

But here is the irony of history: the hegemony of the United States was dependent on its national dominance in the world economy and global leadership on the path of modernization. And the very success of global capitalism has now turned against that nation that most effectively spread its influence worldwide.

Enter Donald Trump...

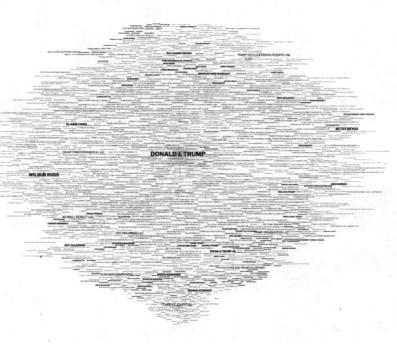

5. The Irony of History

Many of the methods that the United States used against others during its years of hegemony are now being introduced at home. When it comes to the distortions in power caused by neoliberalism, the United States is now catching up with the rest of the world. First, consider the election process itself. Without a doubt, the Russian government interfered with the 2016 democratic elections in the United States, benefitting Trump over Hillary Clinton. I am not happy with the outcome. But one can hardly cry, "UNFAIR!" without acknowledging the hypocrisy. The CIA, since its founding in 1947, has consistently interfered with democratic outcomes in elections abroad, not only in Chile, not only in Poland, not only in Santo Domingo, but also disastrously in 1953, when it orchestrated the overthrow of Mossadeq's democratically elected government in Iran.

We in the United States are experiencing the loss of control over our national economy due to its integration into the global economy—echoing what so many other countries have already experienced. This loss of control has been cited as what motivated many working-class people to vote for Trump. But Trump's promises are in direct contrast to his personal economic situation.

Left: Using data pulled from BuzzFeed's investigation into Trump's more than 1,500 business connections, designer Kim Albrecht created this visualization of his network

Trump's own global network of business connections makes clear that building a protective wall around the US economy is a fantasy, and he knows it. Authoritarian national regimes within a hyper-neoliberal system of capitalism are a danger to global peace that must be taken seriously. It is why I remain convinced that the only possible resistance to both must be devoted to a global humanity in the most inclusive understanding of the term.

Whereas the corporate director of General Motors, Charles Erwin Wilson, could say in the 1950s, with reason, that "what's good for General Motors is good for the USA," today, when right-wing populist Donald Trump says he is going to make America great again, what that slogan indicates is his desire to turn the US government itself into a corporation. This is a hostile takeover by corporate capitalism of a democratically constituted state. Under the cover of antibureaucratic reform, federal government programs are to be either destroyed outright or their activities outsourced to private companies, and federal policies will be judged by market values. Of course, this ignores the very raison d'être of the federal bureaucracy, which has expanded because of the increasing imperative to control capitalist enterprises, not to become one.

Interestingly, there is a precedent even for this.

> The Malaysian Incorporated and Privatization concepts call for all of us to start formulating and adopting a common national corporate philosophy and strategy for action. The time has come for all managers in the private sector to stop thinking of progress and development only in terms of what their own companies and firms intend to do. All must now start thinking in terms of contributing to the well being of the nation as part of their responsibility. Malaysia's future depends on improved productivity and the ability to sell more and more goods to the world. The private sector and the people as a whole must now play their part.
> —Based on a quote from Tun Dr. Mahathir Mohamad

Three decades ago, in the 1980s, the prime minister of Malaysia, Mahathir Mohamad, proposed explicitly that the model for his country's government should be that of a corporation. "Malaysia Inc." was the name for national unity, while trade unions were sidelined and public industries underwent privatization.[9] The same approach was taken by the government of Thailand—still a monarchy—after experiencing economic collapse in the late 1990s. When Thaksin Shinawatra, leader of the Thai Rak Thai ("Thais Love Thais," TRT) Party, was elected

---

9. See the PhD dissertation of Fiona Lee, "Reading Nation in Translation: The Spectral Transnationality of the Malaysian Racial Imaginary," (CUNY Graduate Center, New York, 2014).

prime minister in 2001, he applied the principles of "new management" to governing the country, with himself as Thailand's CEO and the citizens as his "employees." His policy was maximum growth in income and profits, through privatization and strict fiscal discipline.[10]

In Thaksin's words:

> A company is a country. A country is a company. They are the same thing. The management is the same. It is management by economics. From now onwards, this is the era of management by economics, not management by other means. Economics is the deciding factor.

In March 2017, Trump's son-in-law, Jared Kushner, announced that the goal of the administration would be to run the US government like a "great American company": "Our hope is that we can achieve success and efficiencies for our customers, who are the citizens." We are told that in the United States, a 230-year-old democracy, the category of citizen is to be eradicated and replaced by that of "customer"—and this at a time when CEOs are increasingly more concerned with attracting investors than pleasing, or even having, customers. This shift to making profits by attracting investors is modeled on finance capitalism, as opposed to earlier industrial forms—such as Fordism, for example, the aim of which was to attract working-class customers by selling them affordable cars. In comparison with Kushner's version of the corporate model, Thaksin's description of citizens as employees might seem progressive. But the larger point is this: the resources of every nation state—its labor, production, taxation, raw materials—are being pressured politically toward enhancing that nation's competitive position within the system of global capitalism. And this trajectory is being followed regardless of the costs: increasing economic inequality, compromised social welfare, long-term ecological deterioration, and competitive cultural practices that value, above all, winning out over others. If we look at the situation in this way, then even communist China is not an exception to these tendencies. Human needs that are incompatible with the competitive model are sidelined, as citizens are mobilized for realizing the nation state's economic advantage over other global players in this new Olympics of human survival. But the nation as a whole does not share equally in the bounty of victory. Moreover, the winners—a small minority—who truly benefit from the global system are often strikingly lacking in loyalty to their own nations' populations. Citizens, rightly, feel angry. Authoritarianism is the compromised result.

---

10.   See the PhD dissertation of Puangchon Unchanam, "The Bourgeois Crown: Capitalism and the Monarchy in Thailand, 1946–2016," (CUNY Graduate Center, New York, 2017).

Let us sum up the major point: national populations are losing control, not only over capital but over the social commitments of their governments as well. Under these conditions, politicians appeal to nationalism in an attempt to deflect attention from real structural inequalities by fostering an exclusionist, racist, and anti-immigrant response within domestic politics, undermining the powerful global solidarity that resistance movements in the past decades have in fact achieved.

Meanwhile, the rich are getting richer and the poor poorer, worldwide. Democracy has succeeded in one aspect. The rich are now multinational, multiracial, and multicultural. This thin sliver of humanity is spread increasingly across the globe as national elites everywhere are pulled into global networks of power.

The data on global inequality makes clear that non-Western countries have made significant inroads into Western capitalist hegemony. But what are the political costs of treating territories as anthropomorphized forms of national identities, when behind these abstractions, domestic populations are judged as assets or liabilities in accord with their contribution to the corporate model that has refigured the nation state itself?

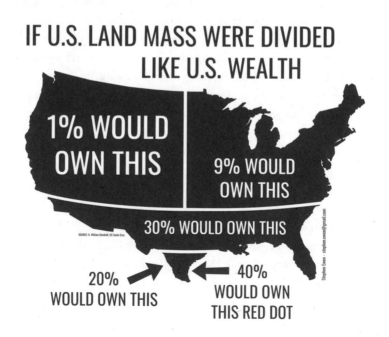

Protest poster by Stephen Ewen, who draws on Thomas Jefferson's equation of land holding with wealth holding, and his concern that land would become so unequally divided that it could threaten the cohesion and stability of the new nation he had recently helped found.

The Chinese government claims to be different, asserting that it has not given up social-ist values as it ascends to the pinnacle of global capitalist power, yet its income inequality has risen sharply. "Communist" billionaires lead lifestyles indistinguishable from the rest of the richest 1 percent that owns 82 percent of the world's wealth.[11]

If, in the past, "two cultures" referred to the mindset of science versus that of the arts and humanities (as C. P. Snow argued famously in 1959), today, the two cultures are economi-cally defined. One is inhabited by those at the top of the economic scale, who travel the globe freely. Their bodies move with ease in and out of gated communities. Their money exits digi-tally to the safety of tax havens abroad. They share with each other luxury resorts, private jets, fashions of dress—and, via marriage and procreation, their DNA. National governments are their instruments for capital gain, as increasingly, the national political elite and the global financial elite have become brethren, if not one and the same.

The second culture, comprising the rest of the world's population, is bound together objectively by the economic conditions of existence: their lives are precarious, fungible, and potentially expendable. But in this case, national boundaries are partitions that cut off aware-ness of their shared situation, and social commonalities are transformed into competitive hostilities. So long as historical events happen to people over their heads, rather than as the

---

11.   These 2018 figures compiled by Oxfam show an uptick of $762 billion of wealth—enough to end extreme poverty
       in the world seven times over: Sam Meredith, "Inequality Gap Widens as 'World's Richest 1% Get 82% of the
       Wealth,' Oxfam Says," CNBC, January 22, 2018, https://www.cnbc.com/2018/01/22/wef-18-oxfam-says-worlds-
       richest-1-percent-get-82-percent-of-the-wealth.html.

consequence of what they are able to do together, the contradiction between nation state and global economy will continue to distort their political freedoms, threaten their livelihoods, and buy off their resistance through the neoliberal promise of individualized salvation or the nationalist fantasy of going it alone. In the global sport of capitalist competition, even the winners are chronically insecure. Authoritarian populism threatens to draw nationally divided people into a Third World War, while the environmental and economic crises that we face make it imperative for us to think and act together across every line of difference.

Capitalism on its own cannot be relied upon for the organization of a good society. Market forces do not by themselves provide a social bond—as we see very clearly from the recent failures of the European Union to turn economic interdependence into political solidarity. The global dominance of the profit motive as the highest goal is not good for people or for any living thing. And so we still need a revolution, lots of them. But how will the idea of *revolution* survive the passing of that modernity to which it has owed its political life? From recent history, what lessons can be learned in order to answer the question: What to do?

6. Revolution Today

Inscription over the main staircase of the entryway of the Humboldt Universität, Berlin

"Philosophers have only always interpreted the world
in various ways; the point is, to change it."

—*Eleventh Thesis on Feuerbach,* **Karl Marx, 1845**

n 1845 Karl Marx outlined eleven theses that critiqued the left Hegelian philosophy for not going far enough, and called for a transformation of theory into practice. What follows here are theses that emulate his number. They originate not from philosophy but from historical experiences of the recent past. They hold up the principles of revolutionary theory to the test of empirical events. If this shows us what Marx, the great modernist thinker, got wrong, that is not itself a cause for pessimism. It is new knowledge of a kind that is handy for revolutionaries today.

49

1. The nation is the place of citizen power, but not itself the revolutionary goal.

Insofar as democratic power is established today, it is limited structurally to national institutions. But leftists will need to overcome this spatial ordering along territorial lines. Yes, we need to take power within nation-state governments, but not for national*ist* goals. Rather, our program must speak to a global agenda—against war, against labor exploitation, against racism and patriarchy, against environmental degradation. National politics must be implemented for planetary political ends. This trans-local perspective defines the left today.

In our time of global insecurity, this larger commitment may seem counterintuitive, given the way populations in fact behave. After all, it is not only the left that holds demonstrations in public spaces. But limiting the base of support to one country will not allow these groups to capture the global imagination that matters in the twenty-first century.

Patriotic Europeans Against the Islamization of the Occident (Pegida) demonstration in Dresden, Germany, January 5, 2015. The signs read as follows: Left: "Citizen Putin, help us, save us! From the corrupt, Volk-hostile regime of the German Republic as well as from America and Israel." Center: "German Volk: Stop the death of the Volk and the betrayal of the homeland." Right: "German families stand for 500 Euros for each child of our German families, tax-free marriages, salaries for mothers."

But history demonstrates that in the face of existential threats, populations can achieve remarkable solidarity across national lines. In 1999, in one month's time, earthquakes hit two countries that had perceived of each other as enemies, first Turkey, in the Marmara region, and then Greece, in the capital of Athens. When the Turks were devastated, a wide swath of Greek municipalities—Athens, Thessaloniki, Piraeus, Patras, Herakleion—side-stepped national governments and responded immediately with aid. A month later, Turks were in Athens, rescuing people from the new earthquake's rubble.[12] Such examples provide the model for trans-local solidarity. When financial crises hit populations like a tsunami, when banks trap lenders and a whole country pays, when government-launched bombs produce a tidal wave of refugees, these are not natural events. They are human-made disasters, and they are just as surely out of the human victims' control. Nationalist rhetoric claims otherwise, blames the victim, and effectively blocks the global possibility of change.

2. Marxist revolutions have not happened in "advanced" economies.

Marxist revolutions have had their greatest successes in what were then nonindustrialized countries: Russia, China, and Cuba. They succeeded because they met urgent and local demands of the people. The Bolshevik Revolution provides the example. Prior to the 1917 revolution in Russia, there was no sizeable working class, even in the major cities. Workers were interpellated into existence as a class by the Bolshevik Party. Wage laborers who could be spared in the Russian wartime economy had been conscripted as soldiers in World War I, and it was the war that produced the realities of the revolutionary situation. The success of the Bolsheviks was made possible by adopting the socialist-agrarian program of the Socialist Revolutionaries, who won the plurality of the national vote in 1917. Theirs was a call for PEACE, BREAD, and LAND.

Russian troops awaiting German attack in the trenches

---

12.   Millions watched as the TV announcer exclaimed: "It's the Turks! They've got the little boy. They saved him." Stephen Kinzer, "Earthquakes Help Warm Greek-Turkish Relations," *New York Times*, September 13, 1999, https://www.nytimes.com/1999/09/13/world/earthquakes-help-warm-greek-turkish-relations.html?n=Top%2F-News%2FScience%2FTopics%2FBirds.

№ 208.
Пятница,
27 октября 1917 г.

ЦѢНА:
въ Петроградѣ 15 коп.
по ст. жел. д. 18 коп.

ИЗВѢСТІЯ
Центральнаго Исполнительнаго Комитета
и петроградскаго совѣта
РАБОЧИХЪ и СОЛДАТСКИХЪ ДЕПУТАТОВЪ.

Адресъ конторы: Логовая, Сибихъ пер. д. № 6. Телефонъ № 218-47.
Адресъ редакціи: Смольный Институтъ, 3-й этажъ комната № 14А. Телефонъ № 16-99.

Декретъ о мирѣ,

принятый единогласно на засѣданіи Все-российскаго Съѣзда Совѣтовъ Рабочихъ, Солдатскихъ и Крестьянскихъ Депутатовъ 26 октября 1917 г.

When the Bolshevik Revolution took place, the first act of the new government was to declare peace.

March 3, 1918: Russian and German troops fraternizing upon the news of an armistice with the Germans, worked out by Trotsky

Women's Day demonstration for bread, Petrograd, March 8, 1917. Signs read: "A Woman's Place is in the Constituent Assembly," "Unity Makes Strength," and "Female Citizens of a Free Russia Demand Electoral Rights."

The demonstration for bread on Women's Day, March 8, 1917, included women's demand for electoral rights. The Bolshevik decree on land, announced in *Izvestia*, responded to peasant concerns.

"Decree on Land," guaranteeing self-sustenance for the predominantly agricultural workers' population, was a socialist revolutionary demand taken over by Lenin

3. There is no blueprint of history.

There are no necessary stages of history, and therefore judgments on political actions in terms of their being either advanced or backward are not justified. But this also means that the failed attempts at social transformation are not disproven because of historical defeat. The revolutions that have succeeded, even if not in the most advanced countries, have at times contained elements more radically human than the modernist model.[13] Valuable elements of revolutions achieved by people acting together that the dominant paradigm considers untimely are evidence that the shaping of revolutionary transformation is a collective task. Collective creativity that imagines new forms of social life is not a luxury of revolutionary change but a vital part of the process.

4. Revolutionary practice is a laboratory (experimentation, not vanguardism)

In the early years of the Bolshevik Revolution, creative cadres were given great freedom and financial support for experimenting with different forms of production, bringing revolutionary imagination into daily use. Here are some examples.

Kazimir Malevich, design for a teapot in the shape of a locomotive

Tbe basic geometric shapes became symbols of socialist society and the hallmark of revolutionary sensibility. To celebrate the first anniversary of the October Revolution, Nathan Altman's design for street art merged abstract and historical forms as a revolutionary reimagining of public space. Artists worked with the local porcelain factories to bring the modern forms into daily life.

---

13.   See Massimiliano Tomba, *Insurgent Universality: An Alternative Legacy of Modernity* (New York: Oxford University Press, 2019).

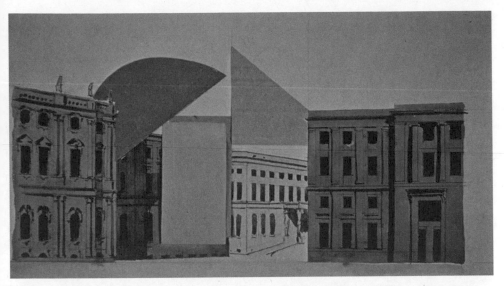

Nathan Altman: Street art, Uritskii Square, first anniversary of the October Revolution, 1918

Nikolai Suetin, suprematist design; Varvara Zukavishnikova, execution: cup and saucer in red and black, porcelain factory product, 1923

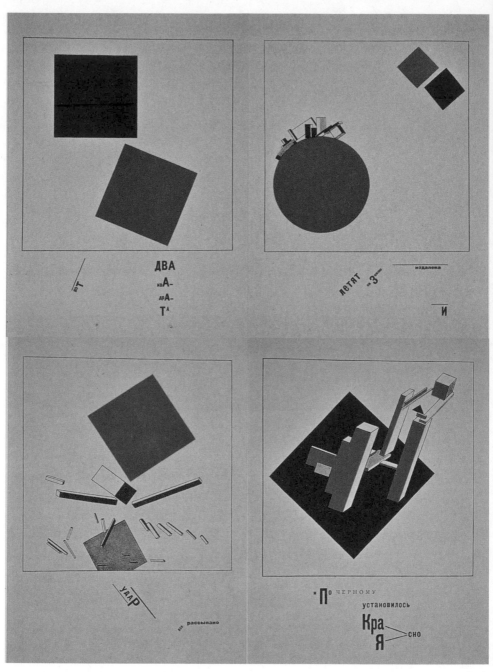

El Lissitzky, children's book: *About Two Squares* (UNOVIS 1922)

As part of the art group UNOVIS, El Lissitzky produced a children's book that told the story of two squares that "fly to Earth from far away." This animation of geometric abstraction brought to a new generation the forms of the new world that would be constructed on the ruins of the old.

The book's full text reads:

here ARE
................two
..............squares
flying toward the Earth
......................................from far away
and see
..............the black restlessly
craSH —
— scattering everywhere
and upon the black
.... the Red
establishes itself clearly
So it ends
................further on

The Agitprop train, bringing culture to the people, was the idea of Alexi Bogdanov—a feminist and a believer in proto-cybernetics and eternal youth. In the 1930s, Bogdanov was in the anti-Stalinist underground movement. There is a return of interest in his ideas today.

Agitprop train

57

Left: Constructivist folding chair, late 1920s. Right: Aleksandr Vesnin, folding furniture, 1923. A sketch of props for *The Man Who Was Thursday*

The creative idea for socialist production, as described by Alexander Rodchenko, was that socialist objects would lack the fetish character of capitalist commodities as criticized by Marx. Rodchenko described the objects' interactive relationship with people as one of товарищи (comrades), adapting with us in our daily lives.

The pattern pieces for Alexander Tatlin's design for a worker's coat were printed in the newspaper *New Daily Life*, to be cut out and applied to fabric for construction in the home.

Pattern for everyday clothes, Alexander Tatlin

Rodchenko's design for a workers' reading room, exhibited in Paris in 1925, had chairs, the arms of which were perfectly positioned for resting the elbows while holding open the newspaper.

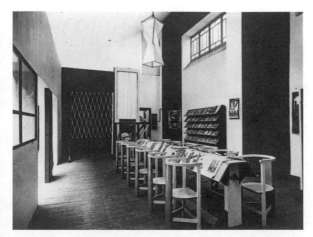

Alexander Rodchenko, workers' reading room, 1925

Maquette for a statue of Karl Marx. Design by Boris Korolev, 1919, and Soviet portrait of Karl Marx

Korolev's radical design for a statue of Karl Marx was never allowed to be constructed. Instead, Karl Marx's official poster is on the right, a rendition that looks like it belongs in a bourgeois Victorian living room:

Bourgeois living room

5. Historical development is not automatically progress.

During the Occupy movements in 2012, which were inspired by the movements of the Spanish Indignados and the Arab Spring, Walter Benjamin's words were cited repeatedly as a form of revolutionary graffiti:

"Marx said revolutions were the locomotives of history; perhaps it is otherwise,
the reaching of humanity riding in that train for the emergency brake."

—*On the Concept of History* (**1940**)

"Záchrana" in Czech—"rescue" in English

Benjamin was perhaps the most consequential theorist of revolution who rejected the Hegelian-Marxist theory of history-as-progress. Yet—this is what my book *YEAR 1* (The MIT Press, forthcoming, 2020) is about—we need historical knowledge now more than ever. If revolution is an idea, not in Hegel's meaning of the idea-realized-in-history but in the premodern, *transcendent* sense—even a Platonic form, even a theological hope—then empirical history remains open to redemption. I can only gesture toward the power of the past that I am speaking about, and hence what such a rescue might mean, in this montage of past and present. →

The eighteenth-century geometric forms used to articulate astronomical connections with the Earth come back to us in the Bolshevik culture's revolutionary imagination.

Samrat Yantra, eighteenth-century sundial, Jantar Mantar, Jaipur, India, juxtaposed to Nathan Altman's street design for the first anniversary of the Bolshevik Revolution, 1918

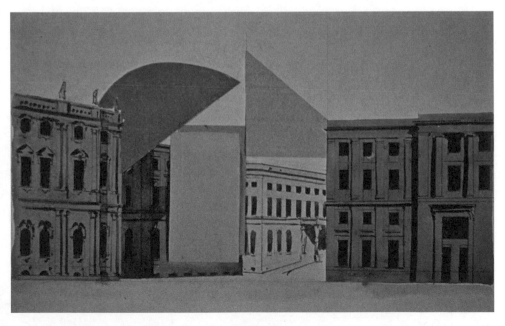

"When I give food to the poor, they call me a saint. When I ask why they are poor, they call me a communist."

—Hélder Câmara

Hélder Câmara, Brazilian liberation theologist

Not only revolutionary aesthetic forms provide a rescue of the past. Revolutionary practice can do that as well, as shown by Hélder Câmara, speaking a discourse of liberation theology as a powerful movement for social change. The implications of such rescue operations performed on the past are wide-ranging, and they are visible throughout the globe.

Let me make this point as clearly as possible. I am rejecting Marx's impatience with the past historical forms, which he called the "muck of the ages" that weigh "like a nightmare" on the backs of revolutionaries in the present.[14] I want to claim that a radical "rupture" with the past is only possible by examining the fragments of history that remain available to us. And that includes the historical fragments of those broken revolutionary traditions of the twentieth century, images of which you see above.

This historical work must be done without Marxist nostalgia for the good old days of working-class struggle. Because we have also learned:

6. The working class is not the subject-object of history.

The working class is not the Hegelian in-itself-and-for-itself of historical unfolding. That metaphysical principle may seem rationally convincing to philosophers, but it is not an empirical account of what has gone on in the past, or is likely to happen in the future. Therefore, as a consequence: there are no primary and secondary contradictions.

Black Lives Matter: "Not a Moment, but a Movement"

14.   Just how far Marx himself can be rescued from the dominant interpretation is an open question. Some of the best readings of Marx today make that gesture, with productive results. See, for example, Tomba, *Insurgent Universality*.

64

Taiwanese LGBT rights activist Chi Chia-wei at Taiwan Pride, 2016

Women's rights rally in Rabat, Morocco, February 20, 2012. The placards read, "You have dislodged us from our land and put us away in the slums."

Liberia: Women for Peace

Race and gender are not merely cultural issues, not merely superstructure phenomena; they are inspiring the most vital revolutionary forces that are taking to the streets today. They lead the way in trans-local organizing that resists the restrictions of left-nationalist goals.

"The revolution will be feminist, or it will not be." Barcelona, International Women's Day, March 8, 2015

The idea is not to replace the global working class as a category with another category of identity (such as Black, women, indigenous, peasant, and so on). The collective is not the universalization of an abstraction. Rather, the collective is intrinsically multiple—defined by the Bolivian René Zavaleta Mercado as *abigarramiento*: heterogeneous, disparate, motley, mixed, impossible to locate on some scale of class or race or indigenous or national identity. In short:

7. The collective is plural.

Demonstration for land rights, 2005, organized by Ekta Parishad–Indian Peasant Movement

April 5, 2016, demonstration in Washington, DC, demanding action on behalf of assassinated Honduran environmental activist Berta Cáceres. At the megaphone is her daughter, Berta Zúñiga Cáceres

Indigenous women in Ecuador protest against a Chinese company's deal to drill for oil in the rain forest, 2016

Coalitions are part of building solidarity with and between the differences. They are demanded by the complexity of our presences. We must move with and beyond the categories that push us apart like center and margin; we must move beyond binaries that separate and divide, and instead find a way towards connectedness that denies unity, or oneness, and instead images solidarity and its tensions.

This is a moment for cross-movement and intersecting actions that will create new alliances that we might not know or imagine yet. This means supporting autonomous actions that become cross movement through the intersections that exist within each. . . .

Right now this work demands a loving generosity with each other as "we" try to find a way to go forward together. Whatever issue you are committed to, make sure to connect with others. "We" must demand everything from each other and ourselves to find the courage together to make a revolution. And making a revolution is a process that has no end in sight, but will create new possibilities.

—Zillah Eisenstein[15]

---

15.   Zillah Eisenstein, "Revolutionary Imaginaries in a Time of Women's Marches," Zillah Eistenstein (blog), February 2, 2017, https://zillaheisenstein.wordpress.com/2017/02/02/revolutionary-imaginaries-in-a-time-of-womens-marches/. See also Zillah's new book, *Abolitionist Socialist Feminism: Radicalizing the Next Revolution* (New York: Monthly Review Press, 2019).

Anti-sexual harassment march on Tahrir Square, Cairo, Egypt, 2013

The specifics of a political situation in a particular time and place produce a composite of political actors, whose *common practice* determines them as organic. The composition of the revolutionary class emerges as a response to a shared consciousness of crisis. Simply put, its composition depends on what people do. Moreover, the solidarity that is produced in the act of social mobilization is the capacity to translate one's own struggles into those of others, imagining communities that do not end at the border of states or religion or ethnicity.

Revolutionary subjectivity is the consequence of conjunctural organization. You cannot know how to act without others, without *seeing* others act. The twenty-first century has already witnessed unprecedented popular mobilizations worldwide; they are in themselves a chain of signifiers, creating solidarity across language, religion, ethnicity, and every other difference. A populist leader as *point de capiton* of this signifying chain is not a practical necessity.

These trans-local solidarities exist. They came first. The right-wing authoritarianism and anti-immigrant upsurge that has followed is a reaction against their amazing visual power. Awareness of other people's struggles is crucial for us today. This is the revolutionary role of social media.

Slovenian solidarity march with the Turkish uprising, June 2013

Occupy Gezi solidarity protest at Zuccotti Park in New York City, June 2013

Demonstrators in Madison, Wisconsin, protesting against budget cuts and the stripping of collective bargaining rights for public workers, link themselves to the Arab Spring, April 5, 2011

Protesters in Minnesota (left) and Baltimore (above) connect the police shootings of unarmed Black people with the violence against Palestinians in Gaza, and the Palestinians return the solidarity. The text (below) of a sign held by Palestinian youth:

I don't know how the Movement for Black Lives would have unfolded had it not been for the fact that Palestinian activists immediately offered solidarity and were at the forefront of an international solidarity movement that further emboldened people in this country to stand up and fight police violence.

—Angela Davis[16]

16. Yakira Levi, "Angela Davis Speech Encourages International Solidarity," *Chicago Defender*, June 26, 2018, https://chicagodefender.com/angela-davis-speech-encourages-international-solidarity/.

Tiananmen Square, June 5, 1989

8: It is imperative that we remain visible to each other.

We are living in a system of global injustice. The neoliberal idea of an end of history, the conclusion of history as a happy convergence of free markets and free citizens, has revealed itself as a betrayal. This revelation is the birth certificate of global struggles throughout the world. Social movements against racism, patriarchy, sexism, ecological devastation, labor exploitation, apartheid, and imperial and nationalist violence are not to be evaluated in instrumental terms alone, as immediately achieving pre-defined goals. Rather, they bear witness to an emerging, shared consciousness that anticipates true revolutionary change.

A word on class warfare: Warren Buffet says, class warfare exists and the wealthy are winning. But the model of revolutionary practice is putting a stop to class war, war's *elimination*, not its perpetuation. It warns us that there must be:

9. No fetishization of revolutionary violence.

Havana, Cuba, 1959. Women soldiers marching in Plaza de la Revolución

Israel Defense Forces: new artillery forces swearing in to the IDF, January 4, 2018

Gender equality is not about equal rights to kill the enemy. Rather, it entails equal rights to refuse the warrior role. All wars, and particularly class wars, are civil wars *and* foreign wars, both at once: the enemy is not, cannot be, neatly divided, and the consequence is physical and psychical devastation that takes generations to heal. *At the same time*—this is what makes the struggle so difficult—there must be:

10. No fetishization of the law.

"Never forget that everything Hitler did in Germany was legal."

—**Martin Luther King Jr.**, *Letter from a Birmingham Jail,* 1963

Martin Luther King Jr., Montgomery County Jail, 1956

The illegitimacy of law is not a contradiction. It is an everyday experience. And it must be called out wherever it appears because the very survival of revolutionary consciousness depends on it.

It was the Romanian-born, Jewish American writer Elie Wiesel, a Holocaust survivor, who fought against the very idea of branding a human being as illegal. He wrote: "You who are so-called illegal aliens must know that no human being is illegal." His image and words recently appeared on the website of the US immigration lawyer Shahid Haque-Hausrath, who works to represent immigrants—Muslims and others—against Donald Trump's xenophobic edicts. Haque-Hausrath writes: "The term 'illegal alien' implies that a person's existence is criminal. I'm not aware of any other circumstance in our common vernacular where a crime is considered to render the individual—as opposed to the individual's actions—as being illegal." This became the rallying cry of the instantaneous movement in opposition to Trump's Executive Order 13769 that banned people from Muslim countries from entering the United States.

New York, January 27, 2018, the night Trump announced a ban on Muslims entering the US

And then this slogan went viral:

In order to challenge the illegality of law itself, the force that is needed has nothing to do with firearms. It is the overwhelming, globally democratic force of numbers across every line of difference. The way to prevent an "end to democracy" is to make democracy the means.

London, February 15, 2003: "The World Says No to War"

On 15 February 2003, there was a coordinated day of protests across the world in which people in more than 600 cities expressed opposition to the imminent Iraq War. It was part of a series of protests and political events that had begun in 2002 and continued as the war took place. Social movement researchers have described the 15 February protest as "the largest protest event in human history."

Sources vary in their estimations of the number of participants involved. According to BBC News, between six and eleven million people took part in protests in up to sixty countries over the weekend of 15 and 16 February; other estimates range from eight million to thirty million.

Some of the largest protests took place in Europe. The protest in Rome involved around three million people, and is listed in the 2004 *Guinness Book of World Records* as the largest anti-war rally in history. Madrid hosted the second largest rally with more than 1.5 million people protesting the invasion of Iraq; Mainland China was the only major region not to see any protests on that day, but small demonstrations, attended mainly by foreign students, were seen later."

—From Wikipedia entry: "15 February Anti-War Protests"

Madrid, 2011

In May 2011, Spanish activists launched the Indignados movement to protest against the austerity programs that had been implemented, leading to the founding of the Podemos party. Five years later: "There is still a lot to do," acknowledges Fabio Gándara, one of the founders of the movement. "The majority of our demands have yet to be fulfilled."

Still, according to Podemos activist Tristán Duanel, there have been some achievements.

"Young people have joined parties," he says, adding that some themes advocated by the Indignados—such as transparency—have now become mainstream.

"But change is slow," he adds. "We have to do something at a European level."

Pastor believes that is beginning to happen, with initiatives such as the Plan B Europe-wide anti-austerity movement created by former Greek finance minister Yanis Varoufakis, or the youth-led "Nuit debout" protests in France.

"We are going back to transnationalism," he says.[17]

17.   "Five Years on, the Indignados have changed Spain's politics," *The Local* (Spain), May 14, 2016, https://www.thelocal.es/20160514/five-years-on-spains-indignados-have-shaken-up-politics.

"Christian Copts were looking out for Muslims while they prayed. Young people were helping older ones. Guys were helping girls and making sure they were fully protected . . . we were all together. . . ."[18]

18   Remembering Tahrir, five years later: Alexandra Zavis and Amro Hassan, "Five Years on, Tahrir Square Activists Look Back at Egypt's Revolution: 'Maybe We Were Naïve,'" *Los Angeles Times*, February 11, 2016, http://www.latimes.com/world/middleeast/la-fg-egypt-tahrir-square-20160211-story.html.

Tahrir Square, Cairo, 2011

"The bodies acted in concert, but they also slept in public, and in both these modalities, they were both vulnerable and demanding, giving political and spatial organization to elementary bodily needs. In this way, they formed themselves into images to be projected to all who watched, petitioning us to receive and respond and so to enlist media coverage that would refuse to let the event be covered over or to slip away. Sleeping on that pavement was not only a way to lay claim to the public, to contest the legitimacy of the state, but also, quite clearly, a way to put the body on the line in its insistence, obduracy and precarity, overcoming the distinction between public and private for the time of revolution."
    —Judith Butler, on the Arab Spring, from *Notes Toward a Performative Theory of Assembly* (Cambridge, Mass.: Harvard University Press, 2015), 98.

Women's March in January 2017, Washington, DC

On January 21, 2017, the day after Trump was inaugurated as US President, six hundred and eighty sites in the US had women's marches; globally, the number involved sixty countries.

"The day after the Inauguration there was the spectacular outpouring of resistance by millions in the Women's March on Washington, and its sister actions. This w as a huge mass action against Trump on the streets of Washington D.C. and the streets of our cities and towns here and across the globe. The marches were incredible and women of color led these many majority white marches. I am not ready to discount the importance of learning from this hugely successful action. If it was not radical or revolutionary enough for some of us, it still offers a fertile site for further radicalization."

—Zillah Eisenstein[19]

19.   Eisenstein, "Revolutionary Imaginaries in a Time of Women's Marches."

11. Numbers matter.

Yesterday [at Occupy Wall Street, Zuccotti Park], one of the speakers at the labor rally said: "We found each other." That sentiment captures the beauty of what is being created here. A wide-open space (as well as an idea so big it can't be contained by any space) for all the people who want a better world to find each other. We are so grateful. If there is one thing I know, it is that the 1 percent loves a crisis. When people are panicked and desperate and no one seems to know what to do, that is the ideal time to push through their wish list of pro-corporate policies: privatizing education and social security, slashing public services, getting rid of the last constraints on corporate power. Amidst the economic crisis, this is happening the world over. And there is only one thing that can block this tactic, and

fortunately, it's a very big thing: the 99 percent. And that 99 percent is taking to the streets from Madison to Madrid to say "No. We will not pay for your crisis." That slogan began in Italy in 2008. It ricocheted to Greece and France and Ireland and finally it has made its way to the square mile where the crisis began. "Why are they protesting?" ask the baffled pundits on TV. Meanwhile, the rest of the world asks: "What took you so long?" "We've been wondering when you were going to show up." And most of all: "Welcome."

—Naomi Klein[20]

20. Naomi Klein, "Occupy Wall Street: The Most Important Thing in the World Right Now," *Nation*, October 6, 2011, https://www.thenation.com/article/occupy-wall-street-most-important-thing-world-now/.

Organizing is the Lifeblood of Democracy

Rio de Janiero, Brazil, June 2013: Protest against rise in bus fares led to nation-wide demonstrations for free public transportation. Banner reads: If the fares don't lower, Rio will stop! Get to work! The National Union of Students (União Nacional dos Estudantes or UNE)

Istanbul, Turkey: Taksim Square, summer 2013: Demonstrations began as protest against urban development plan to destroy Gezi Park. Signs read: Peoples of the World, all will belong to labor! (Struggle Union)The University is standing strong; Tayyip resign! (Student Collectives) Long live the revolution and socialism! (SDP - Socialist democracy party) The factories, fields, political power will all be labor's! (SYKPI) Don't bow down! Now is the time for anarchy.The reality of Turkey. We are coming, breaking our chains. Shut up, Tayyip! PEACE

Moscow, Russia: Pushkin Square, May 2018. Rally against the pension "reform," depriving a lot of people of income source. It was a protest against poverty.

The punctuated interruption ordinary citizens, occupying conscious and connected world, is the solidarity

of business as usual by

public space as a globally

action, visible to the

required of us today.

WHOSE STREETS?

Sudanese demonstrators in Khartoum, Sudan, April 11, 2019

OUR STREETS!

Image Credits

Chapter 1

United Nations headquarters: Arnaldo Jr/Shutterstock.com

Cover of Rostow, *The Stages of Economic Growth*: Courtesy of Cambridge University Press

Ranking the economies: Investopedia.com, July 7, 2017

Thailand, 1997: Apichart Weerawong/Reuters

Argentina, march against IMF: Mario Quinteros/*Clarín*

Lawrenceville protest, September 24, 2009, G-20: TK

Irish financial crisis: William Murphy

Greece votes NO: Wikipedia user Ggia

World nuclear forces 2018: Figures courtesy of Stockholm International Peace Institute

Polar bears declared threatened species: Andreas Weith

Chapter 2

Chile, coup against Allende: Biblioteca del Congreso Nacional de Chile

Stafford Beer / Design: Product development group of the INTEC, 1972–1973. Photos: Gui Bonsiepe Archive, Gui Bonsiepe

Stafford Beer, special operations room / Design: Product development group of the INTEC, 1972–1973. Photos: Gui Bonsiepe Archive, Gui Bonsiepe

Berlin Wall: Reuters

Dreamworld and Catastrophe: The Passing of Mass Utopia in East and West by Susan Buck-Morss, © 2000 Massachusetts Institute of Technology, reprinted courtesy of The MIT Press.

Lech Walesa: Jacques Langevin/Associated Press

Polish election poster: Dole Photograph Collection, Robert J. Dole Institute of Politics Archive and Special Collections, University of Kansas

September 11, 2001, New York City: Courtesy of the Prints and Photographs Division, Library of Congress.

Destruction, aerial view: US Navy photo by chief photographer's mate Eric J. Tilford

African economics graphic: Image provided courtesy of Health Poverty Action

Chapter 3

Rodchenko cover: *USSR in Construction* (December 1934), no. 12

Stalin photomontage: *USSR in Construction* (March 1934), no. 3

Dnieper Hydroelectric Station: Text of caption from Wikipedia; image, *USSR in Construction* (March 1934), no. 3.

Zapatista rebel women: Colectivo Manifiesto

Santo Domingo, El Faro a Colon: Jefry Lagrange Reyes

Columbus Lighthouse: Marvin Del Cid

Tsereteli's statue of Peter the Great: Lubov Tandit

Tsereteli's monument to Columbus: Andre Nunez

Chapter 4

Symbols of This Century: Courtesy of the artist

Proposal for "Billboard for Times Square": Courtesy of the artist

Brasília: UNESCO/Ron Van Oers

Guanabara, 2015: Bruno De Lima/Agencia O Dia/Estadao Contuedo, via AP

Guayana, 2010: Wikipedia user Nils Ally

South End, Hawaii: Justin Dolske

Philippines: Clare Kent

University of Wisconsin–Madison: Jim Farooq for the *Daily Cardinal*

Christopher Columbus claims new world: Chromolithograph print, published by the Prang Educational Co., 1893

Lakota delegation, 1877: Brady-Handy photograph collection, Library of Congress, Prints and Photographs Division

Donald Trump: Gage Skidmore

Chapter 5

If US Land Mass Were Divided Like US Wealth: Stephen Ewen (stephen.ewan@gmail.com)

Network: Image courtesy of Kim Albrecht

What to Do?: Susan Buck-Morss and Google Translate

Chapter 6

Eleventh Thesis: Grace Heraty

Pegida demonstration, 2015: Photo courtesy of blu-news.org

Russian troops awaiting German attack: *National Geographic* 31 (1917), uploaded by Wikipedia user George H. Mewes

March 3, 1918: Heritage Image Partnership Ltd/Alamy Stock Photo

Russian women protest: The State Museum of the Political History of Russia, St. Petersburg, Russia

"Decree on Land": Obtained courtesy of the NYU Bobst Library

Rodchenko, workers' reading room: © 2018 Estate of Alexander Rodchenko/RAO, Moscow/VAGA at ARS, NY

Soviet portrait of Karl Marx: Photo by author

Bourgeois living room: Photo by author

Emergency brake: Wikipedia user ŠJů

Samrat Yantra: Arian Zwegers

Black Lives Matter: Jose Lopez

Taiwan Pride 2016: Wikipedia user KOKUYO

Women's rights rally, Rabat: Reuters/Youssef Boudlal

Barcelona, Women's Day: Photo by Matthias Oesterle/ZUMA Wire/ZUMAPRESS.com/ Alamy Live News

Indian Peasant Movement: Ekta Parishad

Demonstration for Berta Cáceres: Daniel Cima

Indigenous women protest: Mike Reich

Tahrir Square: Gigi Ibrahim

Slovenian solidarity march: Wikipedia user MZaplotnik

Occupy Gezi: Christopher Amos

Madison collective-bargaining protests: Katy Connell

Minnesota and Baltimore protests: Flickr user Fibonacci Blue

Palestinian solidarity: Original photo by Hamde Abu Rahman

Tiananmen Square, 1989: AP/Jeff Widener

Havana, 1959: Alberto Korda

IDF, 2018: IDF Spokesperson's Unit

Martin Luther King Jr.: Montgomery County Archives

New York, January 27, 2018: Photo by Robert K. Chin/Pacific Press/Alamy Live News

"Slogan went viral": Wikipedia user slowking4, Jonathan McIntosh, Lorie Shaull, Beatrice Sandoval, Wikipedia user Cherubino, Image courtesy of Peace Supplies

Poster in Arabic created by Dred Scott and Kyle Goen
London, February 15, 2003: Reuters/Peter Macdiarmid
Madrid, 2011: Rafael Tovar
Tahrir Square, 2011: Wikipedia user The Egyptian Liberal
Women's March: Photo by Flickr user Mobilus in Mobili
"We Are the 99%": Photo by Paul Stein
Rio de Janiero, Creative Commons 3.0 Brazil
Taksim Square: Photo by Lara Fresko
Pushkin Square: Photo by Helen Petrovsky
Sudan April 11, 2019: Stringer/Reuters

Thanks to:

Wikipedia and other open sources
The artists who gave us permissions
Everyone who gave us photos
Everyone in the photos

Index

About Haymarket Books

Haymarket Books is a radical, independent, nonprofit book publisher based in Chicago.

Our mission is to publish books that contribute to struggles for social and economic justice. We strive to make our books a vibrant and organic part of social movements and the education and development of a critical, engaged, international left.

We take inspiration and courage from our namesakes, the Haymarket martyrs, who gave their lives fighting for a better world. Their 1886 struggle for the eight-hour day—which gave us May Day, the international workers' holiday—reminds workers around the world that ordinary people can organize and struggle for their own liberation. These struggles continue today across the globe—struggles against oppression, exploitation, poverty, and war.

Since our founding in 2001, Haymarket Books has published more than five hundred titles. Radically independent, we seek to drive a wedge into the risk-averse world of corporate book publishing. Our authors include Noam Chomsky, Arundhati Roy, Rebecca Solnit, Angela Y. Davis, Howard Zinn, Amy Goodman, Wallace Shawn, Mike Davis, Winona LaDuke, Ilan Pappé, Richard Wolff, Dave Zirin, Keeanga-Yamahtta Taylor, Nick Turse, Dahr Jamail, David Barsamian, Elizabeth Laird, Amira Hass, Mark Steel, Avi Lewis, Naomi Klein, and Neil Davidson. We are also the trade publishers of the acclaimed Historical Materialism Book Series and of Dispatch Books.

© Sebastián Freire

S USAN BUCK-MORSS is a core faculty member of the CUNY Graduate Center's Committee on Globalization and Social Change. Her trans-disciplinary work in political theory emerges out of a constellation of historical material, visual images, and contemporary events. Her previous books include *Hegel, Haiti, and Universal History*, which won the Frantz Fanon Prize Book Prize in 2011, *Thinking Past Terror: Islamism and Critical Theory on the Left*, *Dreamworld* and *Catastrophe: The Passing of Mass Utopia in East and West*, *The Dialectics of Seeing: Walter Benjamin and the Arcades Project*, and *The Origin of Negative Dialectics: Theodor W. Adorno, Walter Benjamin and the Frankfurt Institute*.